Lay visiting to police stations

A report on research
commissioned by
The Home Office

by
Mollie Weatheritt and Carole Vieira

**A Research, Development and
Statistics Directorate Report**

London: Home Office

Home Office Research Studies

The Home Office Research Studies are reports on research undertaken by or on behalf of the Home Office. They cover the range of subjects for which the Home Secretary has responsibility. Titles in the series are listed at the back of this report (copies are available from the address on the back cover). Other publications produced by the Research, Development and Statistics Directorate include Research Findings, the Research Bulletin, Statistical Bulletins and Statistical Papers.

The Research, Development and Statistics Directorate

The Research, Development and Statistics Directorate is an integral part of the Home Office, serving the Ministers and the department itself, its services, Parliament and the public through research, development and statistics. Information and knowledge from these sources informs policy development and the management of programmes; their dissemination improves wider public understanding of matters of Home Office concern.

First published 1998

Application for reproduction should be made to the Information and Publications Group, Room 201, Home Office, 50 Queen Anne's Gate, London SW1H 9AT.

©Crown copyright 1998 ISBN 1 84082 161 2
ISSN 0072 6435

Foreword

Lay visiting to police stations was established over ten years ago as part of the patchwork of arrangements for securing the accountability of the police to local communities. While it is for local police authorities to establish, administer and support lay visiting schemes, they are strongly encouraged to do so in line with guidance issued by the Home Office. The research reported here was commissioned as a 'health check' on existing lay visiting arrangements and the authors were asked to recommend how the current guidance on lay visiting, now six years old, should be revised and updated.

The research was commissioned from the independent Police Foundation, which had previously worked with the National Association for Lay Visiting (NALV) to publish good practice guidance for those with responsibility for administering lay visiting schemes and for lay visitors themselves. The study forms part of a larger programme of work which the Foundation has been undertaking on how the police account locally for what they do.

The report makes numerous recommendations for building upon and developing lay visiting practice and for updating Home Office guidance to police authorities and to chief police officers.

DAVID MOXON
Head of the Crime and Criminal Justice Unit
Research, Development and Statistics Directorate

Acknowledgements

During the course of this research we interviewed more than 100 lay visitors, lay visiting scheme administrators and police officers across the country. Their knowledge and ideas form the basis of virtually all the recommendations in this report. We thank them all for the time they committed to the research and for their willingness to reflect, often at length, on their experiences of lay visiting.

MOLLIE WEATHERITT
CAROLE VIEIRA
The Police Foundation

Contents

Summary

Lay visiting to police stations provides a means by which people unconnected with the police or the criminal justice system can inspect and report on the way which in which arrested persons are dealt with by the police and the conditions in which they are held. Lay visiting was first commended to police authorities and forces in a Home Office circular issued in 1986. Following a review in which lay visiting was found to be operating well in only a few areas, the Home Office issued revised guidance in 1992. There is evidence that this guidance had a considerable and positive effect on the subsequent development of lay visiting.

The last national survey of lay visiting arrangements was carried out in 1993. The Home Office commissioned the research covered in this report in order to consider whether new guidance on lay visiting should be issued and, if so, what that guidance should contain. The report provides information on the extent of lay visiting across the country (which stations are visited and how often); describes what steps police authorities take to ensure that lay visitors are recruited from all sections of the community; and reports on the practical difficulties that lay visiting gives rise to on the ground. The findings are based on a telephone survey of people who administer lay visiting schemes on behalf of provincial police authorities and of the chairs of London panels (Stage 1); and a more detailed follow-up telephone survey of panel co-ordinators and face-to-face interviews with police officers in four provincial schemes, chosen because they appeared to be working well (Stage 2). We also analysed visiting statistics and reviewed lay visiting application forms.

Lay visiting coverage

Virtually all police authorities operate a lay visiting scheme that, on paper at least, covers all the relevant police stations in their area. There is much good visiting practice; that is, stations are scheduled to be visited frequently and receive the visits to which they are entitled. But good coverage on paper also masks a significant amount of poor visiting practice. A significant number of stations were visited either rarely or not at all.

Lay visiting administrators were sometimes unaware of poor visiting practice or, if they knew about it, felt unable to take action to put things right. For some, administering the lay visitors' scheme was but one part of a larger job description that limited the amount of time they could spend on lay visiting. Some felt that the volunteer status of lay visitors made it difficult to set and enforce clear expectations on visiting practice.

The current guidance makes a number of points about effective organisation of, and police authority support for, lay visiting. We think that these should be expanded to include the importance of good administrative support for lay visiting; the need for frequent visiting; and, where panels exist, the importance of committed co-ordinators with a clear job description. We think that the Home Office guidance should be used to convey a more positive and robust view of volunteering, and that these expectations should be balanced by a clear contract of support from the police authority. Police support and responsiveness to lay visitors' concerns is an important component of effective schemes. Again, we think that this should be stated in guidance.

Recruitment

There has been a move over the years towards wider-based, public recruitment, such that schemes dominated by members of the police authority are now rare. Most schemes now recruit at least some of their membership from the public, eight of them exclusively so.

Many scheme administrators doubt whether lay visitors are representative of the community. They are most likely to be aware of the under-representation of young people and people from minority ethnic groups. In only a few schemes are positive steps taken to target recruitment at particular groups. These efforts have had limited success.

There is scope for improving the somewhat unfocused and ad hoc appointment and recruitment processes used by some authorities. A review of application forms suggests that authorities have very different views as to what constitutes relevant recruitment information. Despite national guidance, authorities' approaches to the disclosure of criminal convictions differ considerably.

The guidance should be expanded to cover good practice on recruitment and appointment

Scheme effectiveness

Successful schemes were viewed by our Stage 2 respondents as those which worked at establishing goodwill, trust and co-operation between lay visitors, the police and police authorities through the establishment of careful arrangements for supporting the lay visiting process and responding to lay visitors' concerns. With the exception of a few sceptical, even hostile, custody sergeants, lay visiting was positively regarded by our police respondents. The police would probably have most to lose from any significant weakening in lay visiting arrangements.

Lay visiting was seen as giving rise to few, or no, real problems in the way it currently operates on the ground. The problems that most concerned lay visitors were delays in gaining access to custody areas and escorting officers' introductions. Other causes for concern, seen by police and lay visitors as likely to bring them into conflict with one another, are best addressed in training and, possibly, in a code of conduct, rather than in guidance.

Reviewing scheme performance

Basic standards for the operation of lay visiting are implicit in the guidance and are inspected by HM Inspectorate of Constabulary. There is merit in the guidance encouraging each police authority to audit the performance of its own scheme and also, perhaps, to report on this publicly. Such an audit could effectively start with visiting statistics.

Publicity

Respondents were concerned about the low public profile of lay visiting. There is more that police authorities could do to publicise lay visiting locally using existing channels of communication.

Other aspects of the guidance

Respondents made a number of suggestions for expanding or amending the guidance, particularly on issues concerning lay visitors acting as appropriate adults; the lay visiting response to deaths in custody; the role of lay observers; the use of CS spray; and training.

1 Setting the scene

The United Kingdom is almost certainly alone among the countries of the world in having institutionalised and systematic arrangements for people unconnected with the police or with other parts of the criminal justice system to visit police stations unannounced in order to provide an independent check on the treatment of people being held there[1]. Lay visitors to police stations - members of the public authorised to visit police stations, having random and largely unfettered access to people arrested and detained there and a duty to report on what they find - perform this unique role.

What is lay visiting?

Lay visiting, along with the requirement that the police consult with local communities about local policing, is a child of Lord Scarman's inquiry into the Brixton disorders in 1981 (Scarman, 1981). The aim of lay visiting, like that of consultation, is to promote public confidence in policing through greater transparency by ensuring that policing activity is more publicly accessible, more easily scrutinised and subject to greater questioning and comment. Endorsing a prior recommendation by the Home Affairs Committee that 'Chief Officers of Police should arrange for sufficient random checks to be carried out to ensure that the procedures are properly observed', Lord Scarman added that the safeguards this proposal was intended to introduce 'would be greatly strengthened if it were backed by a statutory system of inspection and supervision of interrogation procedures and detention in police stations'.

Lay visiting was the result. In 1983 the then Home Secretary announced that pilot lay visiting schemes were to be established in seven police force areas. In 1986 all police authorities and chief officers were advised that 'the government welcomed [lay visiting] as a positive suggestion for bringing the police and the community closer together' and of the potential of lay visiting

---

1   Lay visiting arrangements are in place throughout England and Wales and in Northern Ireland but not, as yet, in Scotland.
    Arrangements for the independent supervision of people in police detention are currently in place in the Netherlands and in Hungary. The Dutch scheme is not countrywide but operates in two cities and one police region. Visitors are not 'lay', but have knowledge of, or are professionally involved with, the criminal justice system. In Hungary the Hungarian Helsinki Committee has been authorised since 1996 to make unannounced visits to police stations and report on the treatment of detainees and the conditions of detention.
    There have been various attempts in South Africa to set up lay visiting schemes based on the UK model, but with limited success. There are plans currently to introduce a national framework for lay visiting, but at the time of writing details are not available.

'for promoting public confidence in the work of the police flowing from a better understanding of what goes on in police stations' (Home Office, 1986). The scheme that the Home Office promoted differed in two important respects from that envisaged by Lord Scarman. Lay visitors were not to have access to police interrogations. Nor, in deference to doubts that had been expressed about the need for lay visiting in rural areas, was the scheme made statutory. Instead, the Home Office recommended that schemes be set up 'wherever local wishes and circumstances make them appropriate'.

The 1986 circular defined the purpose of lay visiting as being 'to enable members of the local community to observe, comment and report on the conditions under which persons are detained at police stations and the operation in practice of the statutory and other rules governing their welfare'. Responsibility for establishing and running schemes was vested in the police authority in consultation with the chief constable. Separate guidance on lay visiting within the Metropolitan Police District (MPD) placed the responsibility for lay visiting with the Home Secretary (as police authority for London) and linked lay visiting panels to borough-based police/community consultative groups. Both sets of guidance covered issues relating to the organisation of visits, the appointment of visitors, visiting programmes, the conduct of visits and reporting.

Revised circular guidance was issued to schemes within the MPD in 1991 and to provincial police authorities in 1992 (Home Office, 1991 and 1992). Based on the results of research commissioned from the University of Bath on how schemes were operating (Kemp and Morgan, 1990), the new provincial guidance clarified grey areas, expanded considerably on issues to do with recruitment, organisation and the conduct of visits, recommended tighter procedures and strongly supported the establishment of schemes that recruited from the general public and that were not dominated by the police authority (Home Office, 1992). The new guidance was also more assertive in tone than its predecessor. Abandoning its previous deference to the importance of 'local wishes and circumstances' in determining whether schemes should or should not be established, it stated that 'The Home Secretary is strongly in favour of lay visiting being established *in all force areas* ... He considers that [lay visitors] are as relevant in rural areas as in inner city conurbations' (emphasis added). The guidance also more strongly emphasised the inspectorial aspects of lay visiting, adding to its purposes that of 'provid[ing] an important check on the way police officers carry out their duties with regard to detained persons'.

2

The research

The day-to-day application of good practice guidance frequently exposes ambiguities and inconsistencies in the way it is drafted. Nor can guidance adequately address new situations. And, inevitably, guidance lags behind good practice as it develops on the ground. For all these reasons the Home Office has signalled its intention to revisit and revise the 1992 guidance. It commissioned the research reported here as a preliminary step to so doing.

The aims of the research were:

- to assess the extent and amount of lay visiting coverage across the country;

- to describe the ways in which lay visitors are recruited, paying particular attention to the steps that are taken to ensure that they are representative of their local communities;

- to describe any practical difficulties that lay visiting gives rise to on the ground; and, in so doing:

- to provide a basis for assessing whether the existing circular guidance on lay visiting needs revision and to make suggestions for revising it.

A two-stage review was agreed with the Home Office. Stage 1 involved a national survey of provincial lay visiting scheme administrators and, in London, panel chairs or chairmen. In Stage 2 we focused on a small number of schemes that appeared to be working well and interviewed the co-ordinators of those schemes (unlike scheme administrators, all were lay visitors themselves) and a sample of police officers. The methods used and our assessment of their strengths and weaknesses are described in more detail later in this chapter.

Previous work

Our survey is the fourth national survey of lay visiting to be carried out in the last ten years[2]. As indicated above, in the late 1980s the Home Office commissioned research from Charles Kemp and Rod Morgan to find out how police authorities and chief constables had responded to its initial circular. Kemp and Morgan carried out two surveys of the then existing arrangements, one in 1988 and one in 1989. They found enormous variation in the way that schemes had been implemented and in their degree of

---

2   In addition to national surveys, there have been a number of studies of individual schemes. The early days of the Lambeth (London) and Merseyside schemes have been documented respectively by Creighton (1990) and Walklate (1986), while a more recent (1996) review of practice and lay visitors' views in Devon and Cornwall and Greater Manchester can be found in Ansell (undated).

operational seriousness. Many were 'under-resourced and rudimentary' and in only a minority was lay visiting operating 'vigorously'. The latter were those that: recruited from the general public; operated with autonomy from, but supported by, the police authority, which provided the wherewithal for panels to review and discuss their findings and develop policy; and regularly reported to the authority. Kemp and Morgan's recommendations for improving the effectiveness of lay visiting were incorporated subsequently into revised guidance.

The third survey, carried out in 1993 by Clare Hall and Rod Morgan (Hall and Morgan, 1993), was commissioned by the National Association for Lay Visiting (NALV). The survey sought to chart progress since the issuing of the 1991 (MPD) and 1992 (provincial) guidance and to provide a baseline against which NALV could assess the effectiveness of its own work.

Hall and Morgan documented improvements in virtually all organisational aspects of lay visiting. They attributed this to the guidance which, they concluded, had 'led to a good deal of change and is still having an effect a year later for many schemes'. In summary, they found that compared with the situation four years earlier there were more lay visitors, that more schemes recruited from the general public, that more were organised into panels and that more had instituted arrangements for ensuring that visits took place periodically. But despite these overall trends, Hall and Morgan identified a significant number of police authorities that had not reviewed their practice against the new guidance, or that had done so but had decided against adopting it in full.

In addition to these surveys a broad assessment of the state of lay visiting across the country can be collated from reports of the triennial primary inspections by Her Majesty's Inspectorate of Constabulary[3]. Most schemes emerge from inspections with a clean bill of health but approximately one-quarter do not. The most frequent criticisms voiced by inspectors relate to unrepresentative membership, infrequency of visits and the absence of systems for informing all those who need to know of the contents of lay visiting reports and for taking action on the issues that lay visitors raise.

---

3   Until recently, when the primary inspection cycle was extended, roughly one-third of provincial police forces qualified for a full, primary inspection each year. The analysis that follows covers those provincial forces – almost all – that have been subject to a primary inspection since 1995.

Other relevant developments

There have been three other developments which might have been expected to affect the way in which lay visiting has developed since the 1992 Home Office Circular. These are the establishment of the National Association for Lay Visiting, the Make a Difference Initiative on volunteering and the reconstitution of police authorities as independent corporate bodies with new responsibilities, under the Police and Magistrates' Courts Act 1994[4].

NALV was established in 1993, among other things to support and promote lay visiting and to help formulate and publicise good practice. In 1996 it published two good practice guides, one aimed at lay visitors and the other, more extensive guide, aimed at scheme administrators (National Association for Lay Visiting, 1996a and 1996b). Both guides affirm the Home Office guidance. Both also – particularly the one for scheme administrators – go well beyond it in setting out, for example, how lay visitors should approach their interviews with detainees, what issues to cover during an interview and how to report on a visit. The guide for administrators also covers, in some detail, good practice in relation to publicity, recruitment and selection and training, issues which are barely covered, if at all, in Home Office guidance. Most police authorities and London lay visiting panels are currently in membership of NALV and it is reasonable to expect that its guidance would have had some effect on lay visiting practice.

The Make a Difference Initiative was launched in October 1994 and was aimed at increasing volunteering and awareness thereof. Although the initiative does not seem directly to have affected schemes, we believe it has implications for the way in which lay visiting should be viewed by police authorities and could be presented by the Home Office. We make further observations on this point later in this report.

The creation of new police authorities in 1995 is likely to have prompted reviews of lay visiting arrangements. More than one-quarter of our respondents said that their scheme had been reviewed since 1995 (or, in one case, was soon to be reviewed). Together with the other developments outlined above, we would expect this to move lay visiting even further in the direction of conformity with Home Office guidance.

---

4   Since consolidated in the Police Act 1996.

Research method

The main method of data collection in the Stage 1 national review was by telephone survey. In December 1996 we wrote to every scheme administrator in London and the provinces telling them about the survey and asking them to take part. London panel administrators were also asked to forward the name and contact telephone number of the chairperson of their scheme in order that he or she could also be interviewed.

The interviews were conducted by Carole Vieira during January, February and March 1997. An interview was secured with all bar two of the 42 scheme administrators outside the MPD and a representative (usually the chairperson but in two cases the administrator) of 32 of the 37 London panels. Interviews with provincial scheme administrators lasted for about 45 minutes and those with London chairpersons, where issues of organisation and of visiting frequency were more straightforward or were already known, for about 25 minutes.

Information from interviews was supplemented with visiting statistics where these were available. We also obtained lay visitor application forms from 26 of the provincial schemes (we analyse these in Chapter 3). Mollie Weatheritt (MW) spoke to a small number of lay visitors who either currently served on a separately administered appropriate adult panel or had done so in the past.

The topics covered in the interviews in the provinces were: how the schemes were organised and monitored and the nature of communications between lay visitors themselves and between lay visitors and the police authority; the number of lay visitors and whether they were drawn from the police authority, consultative groups or members of the public; lay visitors' tenure; the number of stations visited and expectations as to the frequency of visiting; and in the provinces and in London were: recruitment policies and campaigns; difficulties in recruitment; and methods of evaluating scheme performance. Respondents were also asked what practical problems had arisen within their scheme that they thought should be addressed in new Home Office guidance; and, in greater detail and at the specific request of the Home Office, whether the guidance relating to deaths in custody and to lay visitors acting as appropriate adults was adequate and workable.

Following the completion of Stage 1, the Home Office asked us to focus on a small number of schemes which, on the evidence we had collected already, appeared to be working well, and to identify what factors appeared to contribute to their effectiveness. We defined effective schemes as those that had consistently maintained a frequent programme of visiting across all or nearly all of the stations in their area and from this group chose five schemes that between them covered urban conurbations, other urban areas and rural areas. In autumn 1997 we wrote to chief constables in the relevant forces asking to visit the force and speak to custody sergeants, divisional commanders and those headquarters staff responsible for lay visiting. Four chief constables agreed to this and visits were subsequently made (by MW) to Cheshire, Gloucestershire, Hampshire and South Yorkshire forces. Interviews were held with officers (chief officer or superintendent rank) responsible for force policy on lay visiting, divisional commanders, inspectors and custody sergeants. Twenty-three officers were interviewed, including 12 custody sergeants. Discussions were also held with two officers from the department in the Metropolitan Police that deals with lay visiting. Discussions with custody sergeants lasted for about 45 minutes, those with senior officers somewhat longer.

In addition we sought telephone interviews with the 15 lay visiting co-ordinators in the four forces. All agreed to be interviewed. Each of these interviews was conducted by MW and lasted for about an hour.

The topics covered in the interviews with police officers and with lay visitors were the same and included: what their understanding was of the role of lay visiting and what they thought the police, detainees and the community gained from it; what kinds of behaviour, by the police and by lay visitors, caused conflict and difficulties; what suggestions they had for improving the effectiveness of lay visiting and for better assessing lay visitors' effectiveness; and whether and in what directions they thought that lay visitors' remit could be extended.

Early on in the research we were advised that interviews with scheme administrators would produce both a more favourable and a less detailed picture of lay visiting than would talking to lay visitors themselves, and that administrators would not always be fully aware of the practical difficulties of lay visiting. This proved to be the case. Administrators, understandably and with justification, saw the survey not just as a review of existing lay visiting arrangements but also as an assessment of how well they were doing their job. Most, therefore, were keen to present their scheme in the best possible light. Although several administrators were frank about their scheme's failings, these were new in post and intended to take action to put things right.

At the opposite end of the spectrum were those administrators whose views that their scheme was functioning well were belied by visiting statistics showing that stations were being visited only infrequently, and by an organisational structure that left lay visitors pretty much to their own devices and without central organisational support. Where possible we have drawn on visiting statistics and on information about scheme organisation and structure to flesh out, or counterbalance, administrators' views. With some exceptions these sources tend to give a less rosy picture of the state of provincial lay visiting than reliance on administrators' views alone. In addition, administrators proved not always to be a good source of information on the practical problems facing schemes. Lay visiting usually formed one part (often a small one) of a larger job description and pressures on administrators' time precluded a detailed involvement in issues that would have been familiar and of concern to individual lay visitors. Interviews with London chairpersons were generally more successful in identifying problems and eliciting practical suggestions than were those with provincial scheme administrators, not least because the chairpersons' administrative effectiveness was not at issue in the way that administrators' was.

On the plus side, administrators were a good source of information on the organisation and administration of schemes and of the police authority's approach to recruitment. As a result we were able to identify a number of issues relating to the organisation and support of schemes which we felt could be addressed effectively in new guidance.

A note on visiting statistics

We asked scheme administrators to send us visiting statistics for the latest time period for which they were available. Most sent figures for all or part of 1996. Readers should bear in mind that our discussion of visiting programmes and the strengths and weaknesses we identify in those programmes are based on past rather than present performance, albeit the relatively recent past.

The scope of this report

The remainder of this report is organised as follows. Chapter 2 deals with the extent of lay visiting across the country: which police authorities have functioning schemes; how many police stations are covered; and the frequency with which stations are expected to be visited and are visited in practice. Although we were not asked to examine the ways in which schemes are organised and administered, we nonetheless collected some information on this, partly to enable comparison with previous studies but mainly because deficiencies in lay visiting coverage seemed likely to be related to the way in which schemes are organised and monitored. Chapter 3 deals with the arrangements that are in place to ensure that lay visitors are representative of their local community and describes how and at whom scheme administrators target recruitment, and with what results. The material in Chapters 2 and 3 is based on the national survey. Chapter 4 draws on our discussions with provincial lay visiting co-ordinators and with police officers to identify the practical problems of lay visiting on the ground and what factors respondents believed contribute to the effectiveness of lay visiting. In Chapter 5 we review the existing Home Office guidance, including two aspects of it that the Home Office asked us specifically to examine – those relating to lay visitors acting as appropriate adults and the adequacy of the guidance on deaths in custody.

We make recommendations for revising the guidance where appropriate throughout the report. Those recommendations, together with other changes and additions to the guidance which respondents suggested, are drawn together in Chapter 5.

2 Lay visiting coverage

We used three measures to assess the scope of lay visiting coverage. First, we asked administrators which police stations were formally covered by their scheme. Second, we asked them whether there existed within their scheme a clear expectation as to how often each station should be visited and, if so, what that was. And third, we collected information on how often stations were visited in practice and compared that with stated policy.

The extent of schemes: the provinces

As a result of the research they carried out in 1993 Hall and Morgan reported that all provincial police authorities had established lay visiting schemes. Most were comprehensive in the sense of purporting to cover all designated stations[1] but four were confined to only some designated stations, those in Norfolk and North Yorkshire because they were pilot schemes and those in Sussex and Wiltshire because a decision had been taken not to have a force-wide scheme.

In 1997 nearly all administrators reported that their authority ran a lay visiting scheme and that it covered every designated station. (In 15 areas non-designated stations were also covered.) The exceptions were as follows.

- *Dyfed Powys.* The scheme was not operating at the time of interview. We understand that a new scheme has since been established.

- *North Yorkshire.* Described as a 'pilot' scheme by Hall and Morgan in 1993, the scheme had not been significantly extended at the time of the interview, when only three of the eight stations were included. The scheme was scheduled, however, to become comprehensive shortly afterwards, in April 1997.

- *Suffolk.* The scheme covered nine of the 15 stations. Two more were to be included from April 1997, the remaining four by 1999.

---

1   Stations designated by the chief officer of police under s35 of the Police and Criminal Evidence Act 1984 as those to be used for the purpose of 'detaining arrested persons'. Arrested persons may also, in certain circumstances, be detained at non-designated stations, but may not be held there beyond six hours.

In addition, we had doubts about the viability of the scheme in the City of London where we had no evidence that lay visitors undertook any visits[2].

Although administrators reported that all designated stations were covered by their scheme, it was clear that not all stations were actually visited. One-quarter of the 75 stations purportedly covered by the following schemes were not visited over the (varying) periods for which visiting statistics were available: Lancashire, Norfolk, Nottinghamshire, Thames Valley, Warwickshire and Wiltshire. And, as our discussion of visiting statistics (below) indicates, we felt that other schemes were operating below maximum effectiveness and that some were teetering on the edge of non-viability.

It is difficult to compare the position documented by Hall and Morgan in 1993 with that in 1997. They relied on what administrators told them, did not have access to visiting statistics and did not attempt an overall, still less a critical assessment, of the variation in the scope of lay visiting arrangements across the country. However, a comparison based on administrators' reports alone suggests that progress has been slow (only in Sussex has the scope of the scheme been extended, although changes in North Yorkshire were imminent) and in some respects the situation has worsened.

We think that this may reflect more widespread problems with local commitment to lay visiting and return to this issue at various points below.

The extent of schemes: London

A lay visiting scheme operates in every London borough and covers all designated stations. Apart from the merger of the Kingston and Esher panels, the situation has remained unchanged since the survey by Hall and Morgan, who themselves report little change in the situation since 1989. In other words, the position in London has been stable for many years.

The size of schemes: the provinces

Hall and Morgan reported that 'there has been a significant increase in the overall number of visitors involved in schemes since 1990'. Schemes have continued to grow since 1993. By 1997 there were proportionally only half as many small schemes (under 35 members) as there had been in 1993. Almost half of all schemes had 50 or more visitors.

---

2   The situation has since changed. The report of the 1998 inspection of the City of London Police states that a 'full complement' of visitors 'undertake a regular pattern of visits'.

The number of designated stations covered by provincial schemes varies considerably – from two (Gwent) to approximately 30 (Greater Manchester and West Midlands). Slightly over half the schemes cover ten or fewer designated stations. Other things being equal, larger schemes will be more complex to administer and will absorb more staff time. Such factors might be considered adversely to affect visiting frequency but we found little evidence to support this. While there were some very good performers (in terms of visiting frequency) among the smallest schemes (those covering five or fewer stations), some of the worst performing schemes were also to be found amongst this group.

The size of panels: London

London panels are much smaller than provincial schemes and none exceeds 32 visitors. Two-thirds of London panels visit one or two designated stations. Only Camden visited more than three.

Visiting expectations: the provinces

We asked administrators whether clear expectations existed as to how often each station should be visited and what those expectations were. A clear expectation existed in most schemes, either set centrally by the authority's staff or, in some cases, agreed locally by panel convenors. However, in four schemes – Derbyshire, Essex, North Wales and West Yorkshire – lay visitors were left pretty much to their own devices to visit as and when they wished.

Home Office guidance recommends that urban stations be visited weekly and other stations monthly. It is difficult to be precise about the extent to which this recommendation is followed since the terms 'urban' and 'rural' are not defined in the guidance and are open to varying interpretations. Overall, however, we felt the guidance was interpreted flexibly and in the direction of fewer scheduled visits than it recommends.

There may be good reasons for this. In three schemes – Hampshire, Hertfordshire and the West Midlands – visiting schedules were calculated according to a formula based on the throughput of detainees. In none of the 22 stations in the two schemes for which we had detailed information, Hampshire and Hertfordshire, did the application of their formula lead to a recommended weekly visit. (The schemes covered such 'obviously' urban areas as Basingstoke, Portsmouth, Southampton and Watford.)

We obtained detailed information about expected visiting frequencies for 28 schemes covering 235 designated stations[3]. About one-fifth of those stations fell to be visited weekly, one-third fortnightly and most of the remainder monthly. Fourteen stations were scheduled to receive less than one visit per month, most of them quarterly.

Four authorities set weekly visiting frequencies for all or most of their designated stations. They were Avon and Somerset, Devon and Cornwall, South Yorkshire and Surrey. At the other end of the scale, the six stations in County Durham and four of the 18 stations in Lancashire were expected to be visited no more than four times a year, and the three stations in Dorset no more than six times. On the face of it these wide differences in local practice seem anomalous. We think that in some areas at least there is scope for encouraging more frequent visiting. We discuss the reasons for this and suggest a common rationale for establishing visiting frequencies in Chapter 4.

Visiting expectations: London

All stations in London are expected to be visited at least weekly.

Visiting frequencies: the provinces

We asked administrators to send us records of the number of visits made to each station in their scheme during 1996, or the latest time period for which information was readily available. We obtained this information from 33 authorities. For 25 authorities information was submitted in such a form as to enable us to calculate the number of visits actually undertaken as a proportion of those expected.

Lay visitors in seven of these 25 authorities met or exceeded visiting expectations and in 13 authorities they achieved visiting rates of around 80 per cent or more. Overall, the average visiting rate was 72 per cent.

These are encouraging figures: in no authority did lay visitors carry out fewer than half the total of scheduled visits to all stations. But this positive overall picture conceals the fact that visiting rates could vary markedly between stations within the same authority. One-quarter of the stations for which we had information received half or fewer of the visits to which they were entitled.

Missed visits matter less where visits are scheduled to take place at frequent intervals, e.g. weekly. But as we have seen many stations fell to be visited

---

3   These figures exclude the highly urbanised areas of Greater Manchester, the West Midlands and West Yorkshire.

only monthly. Low actual visiting rates combined with relatively infrequent scheduling resulted in a significant number of stations receiving fewer than 12 lay visits each year. As we have seen, some received none. Many of these stations were in urban areas. They tended to be concentrated in particular authorities, among them: Cambridgeshire, Cumbria, Derbyshire, Dorset, Durham, Gwent, Lancashire, Norfolk, North Wales, Nottinghamshire, Sussex, Thames Valley, Warwickshire and the West Midlands.

Deficiencies in visiting practice need to be set against excellent performance in terms of both relative frequent scheduling of visits (at least fortnightly) and a high proportion of visits undertaken consistently across stations. Devon and Cornwall, Essex, most of Gloucestershire, parts of Hampshire and Hertfordshire, South Yorkshire and Surrey all fall into this category. Each of the three Surrey custody centres was visited at least weekly during 1996. In Devon and Cornwall and Gloucestershire, both rural forces, 80 per cent of the scheduled number of visits were undertaken (weekly in Devon and Cornwall, fortnightly in Gloucestershire). Hampshire achieved visiting rates of 100 per cent or above for 11 of its 14 stations, a high proportion of which were scheduled to be visited fortnightly. Each of the seven stations in Hertfordshire was visited at least once a fortnight.

Visiting frequencies: London

We obtained visiting statistics for 25 of the London panels[4]. Thirteen of them achieved an overall visiting rate of 80 per cent or over and five of 50 per cent or less. Overall, the average visiting rate was 85 per cent, slightly better than the average for those provincial schemes for which we had information. Where London panels score well of course is on the actual frequency of visits to stations, a criterion which few provincial schemes could match.

Provincial organisation

In 1989 Kemp and Morgan found that very few provincial schemes were organisationally strong. They defined strong schemes as ones that operated on a rota system[5] and were organised into panels that met regularly, reported to the police authority and also met with other panels. They found that schemes that were strong on these criteria also recruited from the general public, and they singled out Cheshire and Merseyside as exemplars of good practice in this regard.

---

4   In nine cases these referred to 1996, in seven to 1995 and in six they straddled the two years.
5   Rotas most usually assign a pair of lay visitors to visit named stations during a specified time period (that is a particular week, fortnight, month, or whatever).

Hall and Morgan found that schemes had become considerably stronger organisationally by 1993 than they were in 1989. By 1993, 60 per cent of schemes operated a panel system and a slightly smaller proportion were so organised to ensure, through operating a rota, that visits took place at specified intervals. Hall and Morgan also recorded 'a substantial shift away from police authority-based schemes towards community-based schemes'. Seven schemes were police-authority dominated and 21 recruited mainly from the general public.

These trends have continued. Three-quarters of authorities now operate a panel system[6], very few schemes are dominated by the police authority and almost all recruit from the general public (see Chapter 3).

Although the absence of a panel system does not, in our view, *necessarily* imply organisational weakness or overall ineffectiveness (there are no panels in Devon and Cornwall for example, yet the scheme achieved a high visiting rate thanks to strong central organisation and support), we think the guidance is right to recommend the establishment of panel-based schemes: in two-thirds of the schemes that did not operate a panel, in our view the visiting records left a lot to be desired. It is clear from our review, however, that the mere existence of panels does not itself guarantee organisational effectiveness and that the panel system can all too easily break down in the absence of good central support and effective monitoring from the police authority. For this reason we think the reference in the guidance to *autonomous* panels is misplaced. Panels should not be so autonomous that they can operate as they please or, indeed, not at all. Nor should they be left to operate unsupported. We think instead that the stress should be on establishing 'effective' panels and specifying a minimum definition of effectiveness. The current guidance goes some way towards this (it recommends, for instance, that panels should meet together regularly); we recommend that the definition of what contributes to effective panel functioning should be extended and refined. We make further comment on this point in Chapter 4, where we discuss our Stage 2 respondents' views of what constitutes an effective scheme.

At this point it is worth mentioning two aspects of police authority support for lay visiting.

The first relates to how administrators perceive their role. Effective schemes were often run by administrators who saw it as one of active management and development and who acted as champions of lay visiting. While this is an obvious point, the importance of high-quality, active administrative support for lay visiting, accompanied by effective monitoring procedures, is not currently stressed in the guidance. We think it should be.

---

6   Defined as a group of lay visitors, overseen by a co-ordinator, convenor or chairperson.

A second point relates to the nature of lay visiting as a voluntary activity. Some administrators commented that it was difficult or impossible to apply pressure to under-performing lay visitors because they were volunteers. In other words they did not regard it as legitimate to place clear expectations on lay visitors nor to take action where lay visitors were failing to carry out visits. While we have no evidence that this perception of volunteering and volunteers is widespread, there is little doubt that in some areas it hampers development of better lay visiting. We think that the guidance could usefully endorse a more positive view of volunteering, set out the principles underlying effective volunteering, stress its importance (in the case of lay visiting) in contributing to the credibility of the criminal justice system and encourage police authorities to set out their relationship with lay visitors as one involving clear expectations and obligations on both sides.

Lay visiting contracts are already in place in six authorities and this practice has been endorsed by NALV. We recommend that the guidance commend this practice to police authorities, and that those paragraphs in the guidance relating to grounds for removal of lay visitors should be extended to cover other areas of poor performance, such as failure to undertake visits.

3 Membership and recruitment

As a result of Kemp and Morgan's finding that schemes that drew their membership from the general public were more likely to work effectively, Home Office guidance now recommends that lay visitors be recruited directly from members of the local community and that they be representative of that community. Recruiting from the police authority is widely felt to be undesirable for a supposedly 'lay' scheme even though it is not specifically discouraged (as is, for example, the recruitment of ex-police officers and magistrates). We were asked to review the extent to which schemes draw their membership from the authority and from the general public, and to assess the steps that authorities take to ensure that the lay visitors they recruit are representative of that public.

Police authority membership

As noted in the previous chapter, police authority-dominated schemes are now rare. Only one scheme, Essex, drew its membership solely from the authority. However, this does not mean that police authority members are excluded from schemes. In seven schemes, all or a majority of the non-magistrate members of the authority were also lay visitors, in seven schemes the proportion of lay visitors drawn from the authority was at least 20 per cent and, overall, 22 schemes had at least some police authority members. Table 3.1 shows the position in 1997.

Table 3.1: Police authority membership of schemes (1997)

Authority	Lay visitors (No)	PA membership (No)	PA membership (%)
Bedfordshire	32	10	31
Derbyshire	35	9	20
Dorset	12	6	50
Devon & Cornwall	90	3	3
Essex	15	15	100
Greater Manchester	105	6	6
Hampshire	68	6	9
Hertfordshire	77	4	5
Humberside	54	6	11
Leicestershire	84	2	2
Lincolnshire	40	10	25
Northumbria	80	14	18
Nottinghamshire	50	5/6	10/12
North Wales	22	4	18
North Yorkshire	59	n/a	n/a
Surrey	45	3	7
Sussex	72	9	13
Thames Valley	53	14	26
West Mercia	100	3	4
West Midlands	120	3	3
West Yorkshire	47	12	26

Public membership

Eight schemes (Cambridgeshire, Cheshire, Gloucestershire, Merseyside, Norfolk, Northamptonshire, South Wales and South Yorkshire) recruited *solely* from the public, through open advertisement. Two recruited only from the authority's police/community consultative groups and a further nine from both consultative groups and public advertisement. Of the remaining 21 schemes, all with some police authority membership, all but one recruited from the public, either via public advertisement (14 schemes) or through word of mouth (seven schemes; in three, word of mouth was the main form of recruitment). In all, around one-half of schemes recruited either wholly (two schemes) or in part from consultative groups.

It is clear that the trend towards greater public participation in lay visiting identified by Hall and Morgan has continued. This trend is reflected in the growth of size of schemes; as lay visiting has expanded its scope, it has recruited more widely. Relatively few authorities bucked this trend, although in Essex, membership remained confined to the authority and in Kent, the

City of London and North Wales, recruitment relied solely on personal recommendation and word of mouth.

Although it is no longer as straightforward as it was when Kemp and Morgan undertook their research to characterise the effectiveness of schemes according to the degree of public involvement in them, we think it right that the guidance continues to endorse the desirability of recruiting from the general public. But it is not enough just to recruit in this way. As we observe in the previous chapter, the commitment of publicly recruited lay visitors needs to be actively harnessed and supported by police authorities. We recommend that this is stated unequivocally in the guidance

Representativeness

We asked administrators whether they thought that lay visitors were representative of the local community. Only one (in Cheshire) was satisfied that they were. Twenty-four were reasonably satisfied with the position but some of these felt that there was room for improvement. Fifteen said that panels did not represent the local community at all. Many identified difficulties in recruiting young people (usually defined as those under 35) and people from minority ethnic groups.

London respondents were more likely to be confident that their panels were representative of the local community, although they too were aware of problems in recruiting people from minority ethnic groups (particularly Afro-Caribbean men), and in recruiting and retaining younger visitors with family, childcare and work commitments.

Recruiting processes

Home Office guidance makes few recommendations about recruitment, apart from suggesting the use of local press advertisements and/or consultative groups. The guidance prepared by NALV (1996b) is a great deal fuller. It suggests, among other recommendations, that recruitment should be planned on the basis of predicted need; that application forms should invite potential lay visitors to say why they are applying, as well as seeking basic personal information; and that applicants should be interviewed, ideally to test their suitability against a formal lay visitor specification.

Methods of advertising and targeting

Twenty-six provincial schemes advertised publicly for lay visitors through advertisements in local newspapers (sometimes charged for, sometimes donated), press releases aimed at encouraging feature articles, advertising and features on local radio and television, and through mailouts to local community groups and posters and leaflets in public buildings. The remainder recruited through word of mouth or personal recommendation or through consultative groups.

Despite administrators' reservations about the representativeness of lay visitors, only seven targeted their recruitment at under-represented groups and only four did so by means other than through the consultative group. In addition, only seven schemes undertook ethnic monitoring of applicants on their application forms, thus enabling police authorities to judge the effectiveness of current recruitment procedures in attracting applications from particular groups.

London panels recruited largely through the local press, via contact with local organisations, through leafleting at public events, through word of mouth etc. London panels were more likely to target their recruitment than were provincial schemes: ten did so, but not always successfully. Some panels had difficulties with recruitment per se and we gained the impression of a much higher turnover of lay visitors in London than in the provinces. It was suggested to us that a centralised recruiting initiative would be helpful and we think that this possibility should be explored.

Improving representativeness

There are clearly obstacles to improving the representativeness of lay visitors. First, representativeness is not an issue for many administrators. If it is to become so, its benefits need to be spelt out in revised guidance. Second, many administrators felt that there was little they could do to promote better representation. They believed that people either wanted to become lay visitors or they did not, and felt grateful for whomever they could get. Many remained sceptical as to whether committing time and effort to creating more representative schemes justified the results, particularly when there were more pressing demands on their time. We have some sympathy with this view; it is important to recognise that better lay visiting is more likely to be advanced by administrators concentrating their efforts on ensuring that, their representativeness notwithstanding, those who currently undertake it do so well and are properly trained and supported.

That said, if the benefits of greater representativeness are to be spelt out in the guidance, there will need to be explicit reference to targeting under-represented groups[1]. While we think that NALV should be encouraged to act as a repository of good practice in this regard, we make the general observation that lay visiting probably needs to do more to 'sell' itself to under-represented groups by using more up-to-date marketing techniques and, where appropriate, by tailoring its message more explicitly to their experiences. In this context it is important to remember that policing impacts disproportionately on young men and, particularly, young black men (groups which are under-represented among lay visitors), and that they are, therefore, likely to have a particular interest in ensuring that it is carried out fairly. Finally, the best ambassadors for lay visiting among under-represented groups are members of those groups themselves. While it is right that the form and content of recruitment campaigns should be devised by police authorities in a way that is attuned to local circumstances, we nonetheless recommend that any future national publicity material be designed to attract those groups currently under-represented among lay visitors.

Application forms

We received application forms in relation to 26 provincial schemes. They varied in scope from those that asked for little more than the applicant's name and address to those designed to elicit more detailed information about the applicant's suitability for appointment. Most application forms could, in our view, be improved. Our observations, including the main problems we noted, are as follows.

i   Eight forms asked for the applicant's maiden name rather than using the more inclusive and appropriate formulation 'other names by which you have been known'. Four forms asked for the applicant's Christian name, rather than his or her first or forename.

ii Many forms did not seek the kind of background information that could arguably be useful in helping to maintain a balance of interests and experience among lay visitors, or assess their suitability. Thus, 11 forms did not seek information about the applicant's occupation and 15 sought no information about the applicant's involvement in other voluntary or community work. Only slightly more than half of forms asked applicants what relevant skills or experience they had. Nearly one-quarter did not ask why the applicant was interested in becoming a lay visitor.

---

1   Reliance on ad hoc, reactive recruitment is another factor inhibiting effective targeting. Forty per cent of provincial administrators said that their recruitment was subject to some sort of forward planning. Most of the remainder waited until vacancies arose before recruiting.

iii Some (although a very few) forms asked for what seemed to us excessive amounts of information (for example, a full employment history), or for information that could be regarded as irrelevant or personally intrusive. We wonder whether this might put off otherwise suitable applicants.

iv *Criminal convictions.* The guidance states that 'Anyone who has been convicted of an offence punishable with imprisonment within the last five years or who has ever served a term of imprisonment or detention may not be suitable' to be a lay visitor. It recommends that applicants provide 'details of any convictions which have resulted in a term of imprisonment other than those which are spent by reason of the Rehabilitation of Offenders Act 1974'[2].

This guidance has been applied locally in different ways, partly, we suspect, because it has been misinterpreted, partly because some authorities have chosen to apply a much wider definition of possible unsuitability than the guidance requires, and partly because it is ambiguous and is open to varying interpretations. It is not clear whether applicants are expected to declare only those convictions (other than spent ones) which have resulted in a prison sentence or, alternatively, all such convictions plus all other convictions within the past five years.

Ten authorities required applicants to list *any* offence of which they had been convicted, including, in six cases, spent convictions. A further four required any offence punishable by imprisonment to be declared, irrespective of the date of conviction. One authority required charges and cautions to be listed and specifically stated that the Rehabilitation of Offenders Act 1974 did not apply. Only two authorities strictly adhered to the guidance by requiring applicants to list only those offences for which they have served a term of imprisonment, other than those which were spent.

Only eight application forms specified that convictions would not necessarily act as a disbarment to appointment. Two strongly implied that disbarment was automatic, contrary to the guidance.

The guidance states that applicants should consent to police enquiries being made about them. That consent was sought on only 11 application forms.

---

2   The conviction of anyone convicted of a criminal offence for which he or she received a sentence of imprisonment of not more than two-and-a-half years, or a lesser sentence, is regarded as spent under the Act provided that he or she is not convicted again during a specified period – the 'rehabilitation period'. The length of the rehabilitation period depends on the severity of the original sentence.

Job specifications and interviews

Only Greater Manchester had drawn up a job and person specification for lay visitors. One-third of authorities did not interview applicants prior to appointment; five of these authorities sought nothing beyond the most basic information (name and address or name, address and criminal convictions) about prospective lay visitors on their application form. They included some of the worst-performing schemes in terms of visiting frequency.

The somewhat ad hoc and unfocused nature of the processes of appointment in some authorities and the fact that the NALV guidance on recruitment and selection has been patchily implemented suggest that it would be useful to expand the Home Office guidance to cover these areas and set out the principles of good recruitment practice. We recommend that it does so. We also recommend that NALV be encouraged to act as a repository of good practice on recruitment. We think that the ambiguous way in which the guidance deals with the relevance of criminal convictions should be resolved and that a more uniform approach as to what criminal convictions applicants are required to disclose, and their relevance to appointment, should be encouraged .

Tenure

The guidance discourages police authorities from appointing lay visitors for an indefinite, or over-lengthy term, commenting that 'the term of office should not be so long that the visitor becomes stale'. It falls short of recommending a specified term, but refers authorities to the position in London where the Home Secretary initially appoints lay visitors for three years with the option of a further three-year renewal.

Systems of tenure have become increasingly commonplace. Hall and Morgan found in 1993 that in one-third of authorities lay visitors were permitted to serve indefinitely. That figure has fallen to one-fifth of authorities and administrators in a further two said that there were plans to introduce a tenure system.

The most common periods of tenure were for three years, for three years with the option of an additional three, or for four years. Four authorities balanced the problems associated with lengthy service and those occasioned by the loss of experienced and effective lay visitors by reviewing appointments at regular intervals (normally three-yearly) while not placing any overall limit on the length of time that lay visitors could serve.

We think that the guidance should continue to discourage indefinite appointments and bring to the attention of all authorities existing provincial practice.

4 Respondents' views on lay visiting effectiveness

This section reviews what our respondents told us about existing problems with lay visiting, and how they thought that visiting effectiveness could best be promoted. It draws on information gathered in the national survey, in discussions with police officers and in the telephone survey of lay visiting co-ordinators in four provincial schemes that, on the basis of visiting statistics, appeared to be working well. We explored the practical difficulties of lay visiting in some detail with the respondents from these schemes. We also asked them to reflect more broadly on the functions of lay visiting and whether they thought these were being achieved, and to describe what factors they believed promoted lay visiting effectiveness.

The role and importance of lay visiting

Our police respondents were virtually unanimous in welcoming lay visiting and seeing it as a necessary and unexceptional part of the patchwork of arrangements for securing the accountability of the police. These were not empty words; in each of the four schemes we reviewed they were backed by careful arrangements – regarded positively by police and lay visitors alike – for supporting the lay visiting process and responding to lay visitors' concerns.

Senior officers were particularly committed to lay visiting, seeing it both as an aid to management (lay visitors acted as independent quality assessors of standards in custody areas and alerted managers to any shortcomings in the conditions of custody and the treatment of detainees) and, most importantly, as a concrete demonstration of the police service's commitment to openness to public scrutiny and transparency of operation. Although we did not raise the issue directly with them, we are confident that any moves to weaken the existing guidance on lay visiting would be resisted by most of our respondents. Kemp and Morgan were in 'no doubt that [from a national perspective] the police have benefited most from lay visiting'. Ten years on, it is difficult to gainsay this conclusion. Just as the police have stood most to gain from lay visiting, equally they would have most to lose from any significant weakening in lay visiting arrangements.

The wholehearted commitment to lay visiting by senior officers was not, however, universally shared by our police respondents. While most custody staff appeared to view lay visiting positively, others were merely resigned to it, not because they were convinced of its benefits but because they accepted that that was how things had to be. One or two were highly resistant to the rationale behind lay visiting and hostile to its practice, interpreting the notion of independent scrutiny of their actions as a slur on their professionalism and seeing lay visitors as at best an irritating intrusion and at worst unnecessary and superfluous meddlers. We doubt that these views are widespread or that they necessarily will be susceptible to rational argument. But there does seem to be scope for addressing them, for example by involving lay visitors in training custody officers, and by providing other opportunities for lay visitors and custody staff to exchange views. There may also be scope for encouraging routine feedback from custody staff on the way in which visits are conducted. We deal with this last point in greater detail below.

While most of our respondents, lay visitors and police alike, believed that the police gained considerable benefits from lay visiting, there was a greater divergence of views on its benefits to detainees and to the wider community. Lay visitors felt that their presence could often contribute directly to detainees' welfare, albeit in small ways, by their ability to negotiate solutions to detainees' problems on the spot. This undeniably useful function is, however, diluted by the fact that visitors see such a small proportion of detainees and that, as both the police and lay visitors stressed, visitors rarely uncovered anything untoward in the way that the police treat detainees. Where they do find fault, lay visitors are more likely to focus on the general conditions of custody (for example, cleaning) and on the facilities available to detainees, such as meals. Both visitors and police gave several examples of where pressure from the former had resulted in improvements to conditions and facilities, improvements which, while clearly benefiting detainees, frequently also benefited the police.

The benefits to the community of lay visiting were perceived as being less concrete. Both police and lay visitors stressed the latter's role in reassuring the community that the police were behaving with propriety but felt that this theoretically valuable function was undermined or even negated by the fact that lay visiting was so little known. While we think it is unrealistic to expect that lay visiting will ever become widely known, we nonetheless feel that there is more that lay visitors and police authorities could do publicise it, without incurring additional expense, by exploiting more effectively their existing systems of public consultation and feedback. Some lay visitors report in public through their local consultative committees, some report in public to their police authority and some police authorities regularly receive reports upon lay visiting as standing items on their public agenda. In addition, each police authority now has the opportunity of reporting publicly on the operation of its lay visiting arrangements in its annual report. We recommend that where they do not already do so police authorities consider exploiting these opportunities for publicising lay visiting, and that consideration be given to encouraging them to do so in revised guidance.

Practical difficulties, points of conflict and issues causing concern

As part of our national survey we asked respondents whether lay visitors had experienced any practical problems that they felt could be addressed more adequately than at present in the Home Office guidance. They reported few such problems.

Three provincial administrators commented that the recommendation that lay visitors visit in pairs was unpopular with visitors and could give rise to difficulties in organising visits; and several London chairs commented that the existing rules on tenure and the three-year break before re-appointment created difficulties in maintaining the size of panels. Several provincial administrations commented on practical problems with the operation of schemes (for example, delays in gaining access to police stations; the lack of awareness by custody staff of lay visiting) but these seemed to us to arise less from perceived inadequacies in the guidance and more from difficulties in establishing agreed ground rules with the local police, and ensuring that these were adhered to.

In Stage 2 of the research, we approached this issue in a different way, asking police and lay visitors whether there was any behaviour by the police that did, or would, cause difficulties for lay visitors; whether there was any behaviour by lay visitors that did, or would, cause difficulties for the police; what kind of behaviour they believed would bring lay visitors into disrepute with the police; and whether there were any other areas of conflict or difficulty that should be addressed in the guidance.

Like our national respondents, police officers and lay visiting co-ordinators identified few practical problems with lay visiting as it operated in their force area. Indeed, lay visiting appeared to operate in ways that were virtually trouble-free. Experienced lay visitors frequently contrasted this state of affairs with a point in the past where relationships, particularly between lay visitors and custody staff, had been more strained. Many stressed that problems of this kind had largely (although not entirely) disappeared as the appearance of lay visitors in the custody suite had become a regular feature of life. This is an important point which goes to the heart of what makes for an effective lay visiting scheme and to which we return in the section on visiting frequency below.

Lay visitors' and police officers' views about the kind of behaviour that caused difficulty, particularly in the custody suite, fell into two broad categories. First were issues relating to the observance or, rather, non-observance of procedures governing the operation of the scheme. Second were issues relating to the personal demeanour and attitudes of lay visitors and custody staff.

Procedural issues

Several of our respondents were able to recall major breaches of procedure, or visits which had been mishandled in ways that reverberated beyond the custody suite and caused considerable upset. Although these incidents assumed a firm place in respondents' perception of the history of their scheme, they were regarded as exceptional. It is probably inevitable that such incidents will arise from time to time, even in well-run schemes, and it is difficult to see how they could be prevented by more extensive or more prescriptive central guidance. The test of an effective scheme faced with such difficulties in our view ought to be the manner and speed with which those difficulties are negotiated locally to a successful conclusion.

Lay visitors and police officers concurred that the procedural issues that were most likely to cause lay visitors difficulty were delays (particularly unexplained delays) in granting them access to the custody area and escorting officers' introductions. The guidance on delaying access is already robust. We think the guidance on the escorting officer's introduction could be more so.

The purpose of the escorting officer's introduction is to explain to detainees who lay visitors are and to seek their permission for a visit. Lay visitors' concern is that the *information* conveyed to detainees and the manner in which it is conveyed do not unduly discourage detainees from agreeing to a visit. We believe that most lay visitors, faced with the choice, would want to maximise the rate at which detainees agree to see them. It is also in the interests of the police that lay visitors see as many detainees as possible. Many lay visitors are acutely aware – as are custody staff – that the way in which escorting officers introduce them can affect the take-up rate.

There are many reasons why detainees might not want to speak to lay visitors – some, possibly most, outside the control of lay visitors and the police. The escorting officer's introduction is, however, one factor within their control. We think it would be helpful if the guidance was to place an onus on the police to introduce lay visitors in such a way as to encourage detainees to see them. We recommend that this be done.

Personal demeanour and attitude

Lay visitors were keenly aware of the kind of behaviour that was likely to bring them into conflict with the police or to cause other difficulties. So were the police. Aside from rudeness and officiousness, respondents cited failure by lay visitors to understand police priorities, engaging in excessive petty criticism, adopting an overly adversarial approach, concentrating on finding fault and trying to catch the police out or, conversely, treating the visit as a social occasion. Criticising officers in reports without bringing that criticism directly to their notice was also seen as undesirable practice. The police demeaning or belittling lay visitors, failing to accept their status and treating them with indifference or disrespect were seen by lay visitors and the police alike as the main types of behaviour causing difficulties for lay visitors.

The line between lay visitors causing difficulties for the police and bringing themselves and the scheme into disrepute may on occasion be a fine one, but it may be useful to characterise it in terms of the difference between rudeness and overstepping the boundaries of what is seen to be the lay visiting role. Factors cited by both police and lay visitors as those that could bring the scheme into disrepute were: becoming involved in an investigation or advising the detainee on that investigation; undermining the legitimate authority of the police by, for example, criticising a course of action or questioning police judgement on matters outside the lay visiting remit; specifying a course of action that the police should take or telling them how to do their job; making promises to a detainee on behalf of the police; and breaching confidentiality.

There is little cause for surprise in these lists although it is perhaps instructive that the list we elicited of unacceptable behaviour by lay visitors was considerably longer than that which respondents felt constituted unacceptable behaviour by the police. That no doubt reflects both the nature - and limits - of the lay visiting role and the nature of the power relationships between police and lay visitors within the custody suite. But it is also instructive that the police and lay visitors were in broad agreement as to what constituted unacceptable behaviour. The high degree of consensus over potential sources of conflict clearly has implications for the training of both lay visitors and custody staff, and we recommend that these issues are addressed during training. It also has implications for the way in which the performance of both groups is reviewed and managed. We comment further on the review of lay visitors' performance with respect to this issue below.

We doubt whether it is appropriate for the concerns we have outlined above to be addressed directly in Home Office guidance. It may, however, be appropriate for the guidance to take a more indirect approach. Two of our respondents, one a lay visitor, one a police officer, suggested that lay visiting be guided by a code of conduct setting out the standards of behaviour that lay visitors and the police have a right to expect of one another. We note that the *Reference Manual for Lay Visitors* prepared by the Metropolitan Police contains a note on 'Guidance on Professional Relationships' between police and lay visitors, said to have been drawn up by the Home Office. We think that this is a useful start (although the note is incomplete in certain important respects) and that revised Home Office guidance should commend a similar approach to police authorities. It might also be helpful for the guidance to outline the areas of conduct that could be covered by such a code.

Promoting lay visiting effectiveness

Much of the current Home Office guidance is concerned with promoting the effectiveness of lay visiting. Drawing explicitly on the Kemp and Morgan research, it recommends the establishment of autonomous panels that arrange visiting rotas, meet together regularly and negotiate visiting procedure with the local (divisional) police. Police authorities are exhorted to set up arrangements so that all lay visitors within their area can meet to discuss their findings and submit regular reports.

We have already suggested that the reference to autonomous panels be modified and that the guidance stress more explicitly than it presently does the importance of good administrative support for lay visitors at police authority level. In general we believe that the existing guidance is sound and has stood the test of time extremely well. Certainly, none of our respondents reported any problems with it. Schemes have, however, developed considerably over the ten years since the research underpinning the guidance was carried out and, as we have noted, it is no longer as easy as it was when Kemp and Morgan carried out their review to distinguish between effective and ineffective schemes on the basis of the two main criteria that they identified: the existence of panels; and recruitment from the general public.

We asked our police and lay visitor respondents what, in their experience, made for an effective lay visiting scheme. While most of our respondents characterised effective schemes in terms of good procedures, many also characterised them in terms of the quality of the relationships underlying them. In practice the two are linked and are mutually reinforcing.

Based on what our respondents told us and what we learned about how their schemes were run, we would characterise effective schemes as those with:

- agreed policies on recruitment and training;

- committed co-ordinators with a clear view of their role and access to a knowledgeable and committed scheme administrator;

- volunteer recognition aimed at promoting the commitment and enthusiasm of lay visitors. That recognition needs to be given practical expression in terms of the amount and quality of officer support for lay visiting;

- a frequent visiting programme, compliance with which is robustly monitored, initially by co-ordinators but also by the police authority;

- the establishment of arrangements for lay visitors to discuss the issues arising out of visits and to articulate and, where necessary, review their approach to those issues;

- good channels of communication at all levels between police and lay visitors;

- open discussion of issues and conduct;

- police responsiveness to lay visitors' concerns, including a commitment to dealing speedily with problems and feeding back the results to visitors.

Some of these issues are already touched upon in the guidance. But most of them are not dealt with as fully as they could be, or are not covered at all. We recommend that they should be.

Visiting frequencies

We believe that the establishment of a frequent and consistently observed visiting programme is fundamental to the success of lay visiting. Infrequent visiting precludes the development of the type of relationship with the police that underlies much successful lay visiting, provides an inadequate basis for reassuring the community that all is above board, and prevents visitors from developing the skills of questioning, listening and making and articulating judgements that lie at the heart of a robust and effective scheme. Given the objectives that lay visiting is intended to achieve we doubt whether visiting frequencies of less than one per month can ever be justified. We think that this should be stated in the guidance.

The guidance currently makes a distinction between urban and rural stations and suggests that the latter might be visited less frequently than the former. We think that a more useful and helpful distinction is between busy and less busy stations and that authorities should be encouraged to calculate visiting frequencies on the basis of throughput of detainees. Some already do so. While we recognise that there may be good local reasons for establishing a more frequent visiting programme to particular stations, we think that there are advantages in establishing national standards for visiting frequency based on detainee throughput. We suggest that NALV be encouraged to undertake an initial survey of detainee throughput against visiting programmes at all PACE-designated stations as a preliminary step to calculating such a standard.

Some of our police respondents suggested that more–than–weekly visits would be useful. We recommend that the guidance invites police authorities and chief officers to consider this possibility where it is considered to be appropriate locally.

There is one circumstance where less-than-monthly visits are likely to be appropriate and that involves visits to non-designated stations. At the time of our survey these were included in the visiting programmes of about one-third of provincial schemes. The aim of visiting these stations is less to check on the welfare of detainees, more to assess the conditions of custody. We recommend that the guidance be expanded to cover this possibility, leaving it to local discretion to determine whether or not non-designated stations should be visited.

Reviewing performance

Basic standards for the operation of lay visiting are implicit in the Home Office guidance and, indeed, are inspected by HM Inspectorate of Constabulary as part of its primary inspection. Such inspections are, however, relatively infrequent. We think that the guidance should encourage all police authorities to audit the performance of their own scheme, explain the reasons for any shortfalls in performance and report on this in public, for example in their annual report. We think the starting point for such an audit should be visiting frequencies and that, at the very least, there is a strong case for encouraging all police authorities to collect and regularly review the visiting statistics for the schemes in their area, irrespective of whether they choose to make that information public. Many already compile visiting statistics but some do not. Without such basic information it is impossible for an authority even to begin to assess the state of health of its lay visiting arrangements.

With time, lay visitors and police authorities may wish to develop additional measures of performance, some of which will be qualitative. We think that NALV has a role in developing national professional standards for lay visiting over and above those set out in Home Office guidance, for example in relation to report-writing and training. If it does so, authorities should be encouraged to assess the performance of their schemes against these standards. We leave open the question of whether there should be external independent assessment of the extent to which schemes comply with such standards, but envisage that from time to time NALV will wish to commission reviews of the way in which lay visiting is developing.

In the meantime there is more that lay visitors could do to review their own performance, particularly in the area of visiting conduct. As one co-ordinator put it: "We're looking at police performance but no-one looks at ours".

We asked both the police and lay visitors what, if anything, lay visitors could do to assess their own effectiveness (aside from monitoring visiting frequency and the pattern of visiting). Several suggested that custody staff should be asked to provide feedback on lay visiting practice, both generally and informally, and more routinely and formally at the end of each visit on the visit report form.

We understand that formal reporting by custody staff on the conduct of each visit already occurs in some areas of the country. We think that in order to be useful such feedback needs to be as specific as possible and to be aimed at the development of lay visiting practice. In this regard we were struck by the comments of a number of custody sergeants, to the effect that lay visitors could be more incisive and probing during visits. We suspect that few schemes make use of constructive feedback of this kind as a developmental resource, and think that they could do more to elicit and utilise it.

While we do not consider these arrangements for receiving feedback from the police necessarily to be matters for guidance, we think there is merit in giving them wider currency through NALV.

In early discussions with the Home Office about the research we were asked to collect information as to what detainees thought about lay visiting. While this proved impractical, in many schemes there already exists a useful surrogate measure of how detainees view lay visiting – their refusal to see lay visitors. Refusal rates can provide a useful starting point for schemes interested in monitoring their own effectiveness. We suggest that all schemes consider collecting and reviewing relevant information as part and parcel of their monitoring procedures.

5 Revising the guidance

Our recommendations so far (which we pull together later in this chapter) have emerged from our review of the organisation and structure of schemes. But we also asked our respondents whether there were any other areas of policy and practice which they thought should be addressed in the guidance. We asked additional questions in the national survey relating to appropriate adults and deaths in custody, and deal with these two matters in some detail below.

Appropriate adults[1]

The current guidance disbars lay visitors from acting as appropriate adults during a lay visit. It says that 'it is not compatible with their role for lay visitors to take on any task which requires them to become directly involved with individual detainees, particularly in circumstances which might lead to them being called as witnesses when the detainee's case comes to court. Even where the police are unable to obtain the services of an appropriate adult ... lay visitors should refuse to act in this capacity'.

This prohibition is clear. But it is less clear – and more contentious – whether it does or should extend to lay visitors acting as appropriate adults on occasions when they are not present at a police station in their capacity as lay visitors.

There are two main ways outside the circumstances of a lay visit in which a lay visitor might also act as an appropriate adult. First, a lay visitor who is known by the police to be willing to act as an appropriate adult might be contacted directly by them and asked to come to the station to act in the latter capacity. Secondly, a person who already serves on a separately administered appropriate adult panel might apply to become and be recruited as a lay visitor. Likewise, a lay visitor could be accepted as a member of an appropriate adult scheme.

---

1   Detainees considered to be potentially vulnerable or 'at risk' (notably juveniles and people with a mental handicap or mental disorder) cannot normally be interviewed unless an 'appropriate adult' is present. Code C of the Codes of Practice issued under the Police and Criminal Evidence Act 1984 defines the role of the appropriate adult as 'to advise the person being questioned and to observe whether or not the interview is being conducted properly and fairly, and ... to facilitate communication with the person being interviewed'.

When we began our research it seemed that the weight of opinion was against people acting as both lay visitors and appropriate adults, albeit in separate capacities and on separate occasions. NALV was opposed to the practice (*Lay Visiting Times,* 1994). And visitors in Brent (London) had been told by the Home Office that they would have their lay visiting accreditation withdrawn if they continued to belong to the local appropriate adult scheme administered by the social services department.

The arguments used in support of this position were largely defensive ones. They are that:

- keeping contact with the police to a minimum outside the lay visiting relationship helps lay visitors maintain an appropriate demeanour (neither over-friendly nor unduly hostile) during lay visits;

- the appropriate adult role has a greater potential for conflict with the police than does that of a lay visitor, and appropriate adults who have got into a confrontational situation with the police may find that it detrimentally affects their relationship on a subsequent lay visit;

- people undertaking both roles may find it difficult to separate them and may thus act 'inappropriately' as an appropriate adult during a lay visit and vice versa;

- appropriate adults may become involved in situations which might compromise their independence as individual lay visitors and that of their panel in the eyes of the public.

Towards the end of 1994 the Home Office announced that it intended to fund a pilot study to test whether simultaneous service as a lay visitor and on an appropriate adult panel did indeed create conflicts of interest. In the event that study fell victim to funding difficulties. Instead we were asked to explore with our Stage 1 respondents what, if any, conflicts of interest they thought would arise if lay visitors acted in both capacities.

There was almost universal agreement that the guidance is right to prohibit lay visitors from changing hats during the course of a visit but less clarity and consensus about what would be desirable in other circumstances. While several provincial administrators stated that there would be a conflict of interest if lay visitors could serve in both capacities, when pressed very few were able to articulate what those conflicts of interest might be, save (in three cases) to observe that lay visitors who also attended police stations as appropriate adults might tend to become 'over familiar' with the police, and (in one case) to comment that it could compromise the public's perception of lay visitors if they were to be, albeit in a different capacity, at the beck and call of the police.

It may be of relevance that none of the lay visitors to whom we spoke with experience of acting as appropriate adults felt that this compromised their relationships with the police. None was at the beck and call of the police; they visited police stations as appropriate adults because they were asked to do so by those administering the appropriate adult scheme. And we have already remarked on the widespread public ignorance of lay visiting, in which context it is difficult to see how lay visitors' independence could be compromised in the eyes of the public. Some respondents observed that it would be undesirable for lay visitors to act as appropriate adults because they were not trained for the role and because the responsibilities and expectations placed upon appropriate adults were more onerous. This is indeed relevant where lay visitors act outside a formal appropriate adult scheme and merely make it known to the police that they are willing to be called upon as and when required to act as an appropriate adult. But the point has little force where lay visitors are part of a properly administered appropriate adult scheme, where knowledge and acceptance of the responsibilities of an appropriate adult, and some training in them, would normally be a condition of recruitment.

Arrangements for obtaining appropriate adults and the problems that those arrangements give rise to vary around the country. London chairs were much more likely to be aware of difficulties with existing arrangements for obtaining appropriate adults than were provincial administrators. In several boroughs they were particularly concerned about extended periods of detention for juveniles in the absence of the availability of a suitable adult. Several panels had had local discussions about improving arrangements, and several panels had considered whether lay visitors should become appropriate adults.

More than one-third of the London respondents saw some problem with this. However, only a few referred to issues of independence and impartiality. They were much more likely to stress the practical problems involved with being an appropriate adult: the need to be on call, to be trained for the role and the potentially time-consuming nature of the work, all of which, they felt, would, or should, discourage lay visitors from taking on the role.

We think that these practical problems are better resolved by those responsible for selecting and training appropriate adults and administering appropriate adult schemes than by a blanket prohibition on lay visitors being members of both schemes. We also think that the wider arguments against lay visitors assuming both roles have tended to dominate the debate and that there are important counter-arguments which have tended to be overlooked. In brief, we see the issue less as one of determining in advance and on the basis of (inevitably questionable) hypothesis which categories of people are or are not suitable to be lay visitors, and more as one of ensuring that the recruitment, selection, training, supporting and monitoring of lay visitors as individuals are such as to ensure that good people are appointed, effective practice is encouraged and ineffective practice or inappropriate behaviour is remedied or otherwise dealt with. If that happens, those who 'inappropriately' combine both roles should not last long, while those who can carry out both successfully will not be disbarred from rendering an important public service.

In line with the above analysis we recommend that the current presumption against lay visitors being members of an appropriate adult panel be reversed in favour of allowing them to act in both capacities, and that police authorities be left to devise local policies as they see fit. While we doubt whether there will be many who will want to perform both roles, NALV may wish to review practice and experience at some future date.

Deaths in custody

The guidance says that the police should notify lay visitors 'out of courtesy' of the death of a detainee in custody. We asked respondents whether they thought that the current guidance was satisfactory, whether they wanted the guidance to require the police to inform lay visitors following a death in custody rather than encourage this as a courtesy, and whether they had negotiated any local arrangements which went further than the current guidance and which might be included in a revised circular.

There was a marked difference in response between provincial administrators and London chairs. Of the former, only seven felt that the police should be required to inform lay visitors of a death. On the whole administrators felt that the wording of the existing guidance gave rise to few problems, either because relations with the police were such that they would expect to be informed of a death or, more commonly, because they had had no experience of a death in custody, let alone one which had given rise to local controversy. Because of this few administrators had had the opportunity of considering the issues involved and therefore reflect upon whether the guidance might be improved.

The situation was very different in London, where 24 of the 31 respondents felt that lay visitors should be informed as a matter of course when a detainee had died in custody and not at the discretion of the police. There was also considerable support, as there was among the provincial administrators who supported a requirement to inform, for clarifying the role of lay visitors following a death.

Many of those respondents supporting the status quo did so because they believed that there is 'nothing lay visitors can usefully do' following a death. We think this reinforces the case for setting out what purposes a visit might serve, what visitors should attend to during a visit and what factors they should have in mind when deciding whether or not to make a visit. We recommend that this be done in revised guidance.

Respondents mentioned two further issues on which they would welcome further guidance: the jurisdiction of the coroner and how this affects the conduct of a visit; and how visitors should report to the community following a visit.

Other issues

There were some issues, not all of them covered by the existing guidance, on which respondents would welcome clarification or further information. None of these issues was raised frequently, nor did they necessarily affect many schemes, but they seemed to us to have national implications, if not now then in the future. They are as follows.

CCTV

The introduction of CCTV into custody suites has raised the question of whether lay visitors should have access to footage. Several panels wish to extend their remit in this way, and some are in the process of negotiating access. Guidance on the issues involved would be welcomed.

Access to custody records

The purpose and desirability of lay visitors routinely inspecting custody records has been the subject of debate at lay visitors' conferences and, more recently, of comment and consultation in *Lay Visiting Times*. The guidance is clear that 'visitors will wish to satisfy themselves that the custody record fully and properly records the action taken in connection with detainees while in police custody'. However, many lay visitors do not see the need for, or are unaware of, the purposes of routine inspection. There is, therefore, a case for expanding the guidance to explain more fully the purpose of examining custody records.

Some forces have computerised their custody recording. Some administrators felt that it would protect the police – and thus ensure that there were no problems in lay visitors having access to records – if the guidance was to make clear that access to computerised custody records is not in breach of the Data Protection Act 1984.

When is a detainee not a detainee?

Some respondents described the circumstance where, following mass arrests, detainees are held for some time, possibly in transport within the police station yard, or temporarily in a holding centre, prior to being booked into a station and formally detained there. Where this has occurred some schemes have negotiated local agreements allowing lay visitors access to such detainees. We think the guidance should be expanded to cover this eventuality.

The role of lay observers

Since 1991 the duty of escorting prisoners to court, their custody at court and their return to prison has been contracted out to the private sector. Lay observers are people appointed under the Criminal Justice Act 1991 to inspect the conditions under which prisoners are transported and held. In many places, police and magistrates' courts cells operate as a shared facility and prisoners awaiting their court hearing are kept in police cells. Some lay visitors panels have requested access to these prisoners but, because the conditions in which they are held are inspected by lay observers, access has been refused.

Many lay visitors are unclear about lay observers' remit and why and how it differs from their own, particularly since lay visitors have had for many years access to remanded and sentenced prisoners being detained in police custody because it has not proved possible to admit them to a prison service establishment. In 1996 the Home Office issued a letter aimed at explaining the difference in the roles of lay visitors and lay observers. Despite this, much confusion remains. We think there is scope for explaining more fully than is done in the letter the differences in role and remit and the justification for those differences. This explanation should be incorporated into revised guidance.

Some lay visitors have mentioned to us that they would like to become lay observers but that the lay observer scheme in their locality disbars serving lay visitors from applying. This is not, however, universal practice. Lay visitors in Hampshire, for example, may serve on both schemes and some of them commented that this had not only promoted lay visitors' understanding of what the lay observing scheme was about but had also benefited lay visiting practice.

We are not in a position to comment on the appropriateness of developing national practice in respect of lay observing. But if it is possible to do so, we suggest that consideration be given to developing a consistent policy regarding the recruitment of lay visitors as lay observers.

Training

The guidance places the onus for arranging lay visitors' training on the chief constable. While recognising that the police must be involved in training lay visitors, some respondents felt that the expectation that the police should arrange it conflicted with the expectation that lay visitors should be independent of them. We recommend that the guidance be revised to place the responsibility for arranging training with the police authority, in consultation with the police.

Health and safety issues

The requirement on the police to conduct health and safety audits may affect lay visiting. The position needs to be made explicit. The police will need to alert lay visitors to the possibility of coming into contact with suspects – or cells – that have been exposed to CS spray.

Miscellaneous issues

In addition to the above observations, we think there is a case for making any revised guidance more user-friendly and less traditionally official in format, presentation and tone.

While not directly relevant to the guidance, some London respondents said that the Home Office should make greater efforts to publicise lay visiting and that lay visitors should be recompensed for childcare expenses. It was argued that the latter would, if not attract, at least not deter young people (and particularly single parents) from lay visiting.

Other recommendations which relate to scheme organisation, recruitment, performance review and the conduct of visits have been made throughout this report. We summarise them below.

Scheme organisation

How scheme administrators view their role influences the overall effectiveness of schemes. We recommend that the importance of good central management and development of schemes – and the need to resource this – should be stressed in the guidance.

The guidance should set out the principles behind effective volunteering, promote a positive view of volunteering and present lay visiting in the context of the government's policy on volunteering. It should emphasise that police authorities have a responsibility to support and encourage their volunteers. It should stress the value of placing clear expectations on lay visitors, balanced by a clear contract of support from the police authority. The paragraphs in the guidance relating to grounds for removal of lay visitors should be extended to cover other issues of poor performance, such as failure to undertake visits.

The current emphasis in the guidance on panel-based organisation should be retained but the reference to autonomous panels should not. The guidance should, instead, set out what makes for effective panels. That should include reference to committed co-ordinators, each with a clear job description.

The guidance should set out the importance of police responsiveness to lay visitors' concerns, including a commitment to dealing quickly with problems and feeding back the results to lay visitors. It should stress the importance of good channels of communication at all levels (divisional, headquarters and chief officer) between the police, lay visitors and the police authority.

The guidance should set out the advantages of the police and lay visitors drawing up a code of conduct covering the standards of behaviour that each have a right to expect from one another.

Visiting frequency

We doubt whether a visiting programme of less than one visit per month per station can ever be justified and recommend that this is stated in the guidance. While more frequent visiting programmes should be encouraged, what matters is that visiting frequencies can be justified. A formula based on throughput of detainees is a useful (although not the only) way to approach this. The guidance should concede the value of visiting stations more frequently than weekly where local circumstances warrant this.

More than one-third of authorities have a visiting programme which covers non-designated (referred to in the guidance as non-charging) stations. The purpose of visiting such stations should be stated in the guidance.

Recruitment

The guidance should set out the purpose and benefits of lay visitors being representative of their local community. It should recommend targeting as a means of achieving this.

The guidance should cover issues of good recruitment practice, where relevant drawing on NALV guidance and/or expanding it.

Publicity material should be designed so as to appeal to the concerns of under-represented groups.

The approach to the relevance of and need to disclose criminal convictions should be clarified in the interests of promoting a more uniform approach. Advice on the provisions of the Rehabilitation of Offenders Act 1994 should be circulated separately to police authorities.

Tenure

The guidance should describe the approaches that authorities take to fixing terms of tenure for lay visitors.

The conduct of visits

The guidance should place an onus on the police to introduce lay visitors in such a way as to encourage detainees to see them.

Lay visiting report forms should seek feedback from the police on the way in which the visit was conducted.

Performance review

The guidance should encourage police authorities to collect and review visiting statistics and to take action based upon them, and to collect and review figures on the rate at which detainees refuse to see lay visitors.

Police authorities should be encouraged to publish information relevant to the performance of their lay visiting scheme in their annual report.

The National Association for Lay Visiting

Despite the undoubted importance of Home Office guidance in securing improvements in lay visiting practice across the board, it is inevitable and right that the development of good practice on lay visiting will come from lay visitors themselves and not from central government. NALV, as lay visitors' representative association, is best placed to articulate that practice and ensure that it is disseminated and shared. NALV guidance may, however, be seen as less authoritative and as carrying less weight than that emanating from central government, not least because it cannot be backed by the sanctions consequent upon formal inspection.

We have already commented on some ways in which NALV could be involved in the development of lay visiting practice. We think the Home Office should do what it can to support the credibility and hence authority of NALV, including supporting its development as a repository and disseminator of good practice and, where possible, endorsing in its own guidance the practice set out in NALV's good practice handbooks.

References

Ansell, Ian (undated) 'Lay Visiting: A Tale of Two Schemes'. Final year dissertation. University of Plymouth.

Creighton, Sean (1990). *Dignity without Liberty: A Report on Lay Visiting to Lambeth Police Stations*. Bristol Centre for Criminal Justice.

Hall, Claire and Morgan, Rod (1993). *Lay Visitors to Police Stations: An Update*. University of Bristol Centre for Criminal Justice.

Home Office (1986). *Lay Visitors to Police Stations*. Circular No 12/1986.

Home Office (1991). *Lay Visitors to Police Stations: Metropolitan Police District Revised Guidelines*.

Home Office (1992). *Lay Visitors to Police Stations: Revised Guidance.* Circular No 4/1992.

Kemp, Charles and Morgan, Rod (1990). *Lay Visitors to Police Stations*. Report to the Home Office. Bristol and Bath Centre for Criminal Justice.

Lay Visiting Times 1994 'Appropriate Adult Scheme'. Issue 2, April.

National Association for Lay Visiting (1996a). *Lay Visiting: A Working Guide for Lay Visitors*.

National Association for Lay Visiting (1996b). *Lay Visiting: A Working Guide for Scheme Administrators*.

Scarman (1991). *The Brixton Disorders 10–12 April 1981.* Report of an inquiry by the Rt. Hon. Lord Scarman, OBE. Cmnd 8427. London: HMSO.

Walklate, Sandra (1986). *The Merseyside Lay Visiting Scheme*. Merseyside County Council.

Publications

List of research publications

The most recent research reports published are listed below. A **full** list of publications is available on request from the Research, Development and Statistics Directorate, Information and Publications Group.

Home Office Research Studies (HORS)

181. **Coroner service survey.** Roger Tarling. 1998.

182. **The prevention of plastic and cheque fraud revisited.** Michael Levi and Jim Handley. 1998.

183. **Drugs and crime: the results of research on drug testing and interviewing arrestees.** Trevor Bennett. 1998.

184. **Remand decisions and offending on bail: evaluation of the Bail Process Project.** Patricia M Morgan and Paul F Henderson. 1998.

185. **Entry into the criminal justice system: a survey of police arrests and their outcomes.** Coretta Phillips and David Brown with the assistance of Zoë James and Paul Goodrich. 1998

186. **The restricted hospital order: from court to the community.** Robert Street. 1998

187. **Reducing Offending: An assessment of research evidence on ways of dealing with offending behaviour.** Edited by Peter Goldblatt and Chris Lewis. 1998.

188. **Lay visiting to police stations.** Mollie Weatheritt and Carole Vieira. 1998

189. **Mandatory drug testing in prisons: The relationship between MDT and the level and nature of drug misuse.** Kimmett Edgar and Ian O'Donnell. 1998

190. **Trespass and protest: policing under the Criminal Justice and Public Order Act 1994.** Tom Bucke and Zoë James. 1998.

Research Findings

59. **Ethnicity and contacts with the police: latest findings from the British Crime Survey.** Tom Bucke. 1997.

60. **Policing and the public: findings from the 1996 British Crime Survey.** Catriona Mirrlees-Black and Tracy Budd. 1997.

61. **Changing offenders' attitudes and behaviour: what works?** Julie Vennard, Carol Hedderman and Darren Sugg. 1997.

62. **Suspects in police custody and the revised PACE codes of practice.** Tom Bucke and David Brown. 1997.

63. **Neighbourhood watch co-ordinators.** Elizabeth Turner and Banos Alexandrou. 1997.

64. **Attitudes to punishment: findings from the 1996 British Crime Survey.** Michael Hough and Julian Roberts. 1998.

65. **The effects of video violence on young offenders.** Kevin Browne and Amanda Pennell. 1998.

66. **Electronic monitoring of curfew orders: the second year of the trials.** Ed Mortimer and Chris May. 1998.

67. **Public perceptions of drug-related crime in 1997.** Nigel Charles. 1998.

68. **Witness care in magistrates' courts and the youth court.** Joyce Plotnikoff and Richard Woolfson. 1998.

69. **Handling stolen goods and theft: a market reduction approach.** Mike Sutton. 1998.

70. **Drug testing arrestees.** Trevor Bennett. 1998.

71. **Prevention of plastic card fraud.** Michael Levi and Jim Handley. 1998.

72. **Offending on bail and police use of conditional bail.** David Brown. 1998.

73. **Voluntary after-care.** Mike Maguire, Peter Raynor, Maurice Vanstone and Jocelyn Kynch. 1998.

74. **Fast-tracking of persistent young offenders.** John Graham. 1998.

75. **Mandatory drug testing in prisons – an evaluation.** Kimmett Edgar and Ian O'Donnell. 1998.

76. **The prison population in 1997: a statistical review**. Philip White. 1998.

77. **Rural areas and crime: findings from the British crime survey.** Catriona Mirrlees-Black. 1998.

78. **A review of classification systems for sex offenders.** Dawn Fisher and George Mair. 1998.

79. **An evaluation of the prison sex offender treatment programme.** Anthony Beech et al. 1998.

80. **Age limits for babies in prison: some lessons from abroad.** Diane Caddle. 1998.

81. **Motor projects in England & Wales: an evaluation.** Darren Sugg. 1998

82. **HIV/Aids risk behaviour among adult male prisoners.** John Strange et al. 1998.

83. **Concern about crime: findings from the 1998 British Crime Survey**. Catriona Mirrlees-Black and Jonathan Allen. 1998.

Occasional Papers

Evaluation of a Home Office initiative to help offenders into employment. Ken Roberts, Alana Barton, Julian Buchanan and Barry Goldson. 1997.

The impact of the national lottery on the horse-race betting levy. Simon Field and James Dunmore. 1997.

The cost of fires. A review of the information available. Donald Roy. 1997.

Monitoring and evaluation of WOLDS remand prison and comparisons with public-sector prisons, in particular HMP Woodhill. A Keith Bottomley, Adrian James, Emma Clare and Alison Liebling. 1997.

Requests for Publications

Home Office Research Studies, Research Findings and *Occasional Papers* can be requested from:

Research, Development and Statistics Directorate
Information and Publications Group
Room 201, Home Office
50 Queen Anne's Gate
London SW1H 9AT
Telephone: 0171-273 2084
Fascimile: 0171-222 0211
Internet: http://www.homeoffice.gov.uk/rds/index.htm
E-mail: rds.ho@gtnet.gov.uk